For: Claire
old friend of Mary Ellen —
new friend of Richie —
fellow writer

compliments of the author,

Richie

A Phonics Reader

THERE'S A BEAR WITH A PEAR!

By Richie Williams
Illustrated by Bodvar Leos

With a Parent-Teacher Guide
by Beth Williams

A Cape Cod Geographic™ Imprint

CAPE
COD
GEOGRAPHIC™

Geosciences Information Services
P.O. Box 911
West Falmouth, MA 02574-0911 U.S.A.
Tel: 508-540-6490
e-mail: *gis@cape.com*

Printer: gallagher graphics design and printing
P.O. Box 778
Cataumet, MA 02534-0778 U.S.A.

Designer: Kirsten E. Healey

ISBN 0–9777100–0–9 (hardcover)

Printed in the United States of America

Papa Richie dedicates this book to five very special grandchildren:

Scott, Eric, Justin, Grant, and Caroline

Key to Rhyming Words in Each Illustration:

	Caption	Hidden words and definitions
Aa	There's an ape with a grape!	cape
Bb	There's a bear with a pear!	
Cc	There's a cat in a vat!	bat, hat, fat [cat]
Dd	There's a dog on a log!	fog
Ee	There's an eel on a wheel!	[banana] peel
Ff	There's a frog in a bog!	hog
Gg	There's a goat in a boat!	coat, afloat [on the water], moat
Hh	There's a horse with a Norse!	gorse [low bush with yellow flower]
Ii	There's an impala at a gala!	
Jj	There's a jaguar in the car!	jar [of grape jelly], tar [road]
Kk	There's a kangaroo in the loo!	cuckoo [bird], choo-choo train, cow mooing, loo (English word for bathroom)
Ll	There's a loon with the Moon!	balloon, lagoon
Mm	There's moose with a goose!	caboose
Nn	There's a nuthatch in a blueberry patch!	[two boys playing] catch
Oo	There's an otter with a potter!	teeter-totter [seesaw]
Pp	There's a pig with a wig!	dancing [a jig]
Qq	There's a quail with a tail!	sail, sailboat
Rr	There's a rat in a hat!	[on a] mat
Ss	There's a snake on a rake!	cake, snowflake
Tt	There's a tern on a fern!	
Uu	There's a unicorn with a horn!	corn
Vv	There's a vole in a hole!	[telephone] pole
Ww	There's a weasel on a diesel!	
Xx	There's an x-ray fish with a dish!	
Yy	There's a yak in the flak!	flak (exploding antiaircraft shell)
Zz	There's a zebra in the umbra!	umbra (shadow)

Aa

There's an ape with a grape!

Bb

There's a bear with a pear!

There's a cat in a vat!

Dd

There's a dog on a log!

Ee

There's an eel on a wheel!

Ff

There's a frog in a bog!

Gg

There's a goat in a boat!

Hh

There's a horse with a Norse!

Ii

There's an imp**ala** at a g**ala**!

Jj

There's a jaguar in the car!

There's a kangaroo in the loo!

Ll

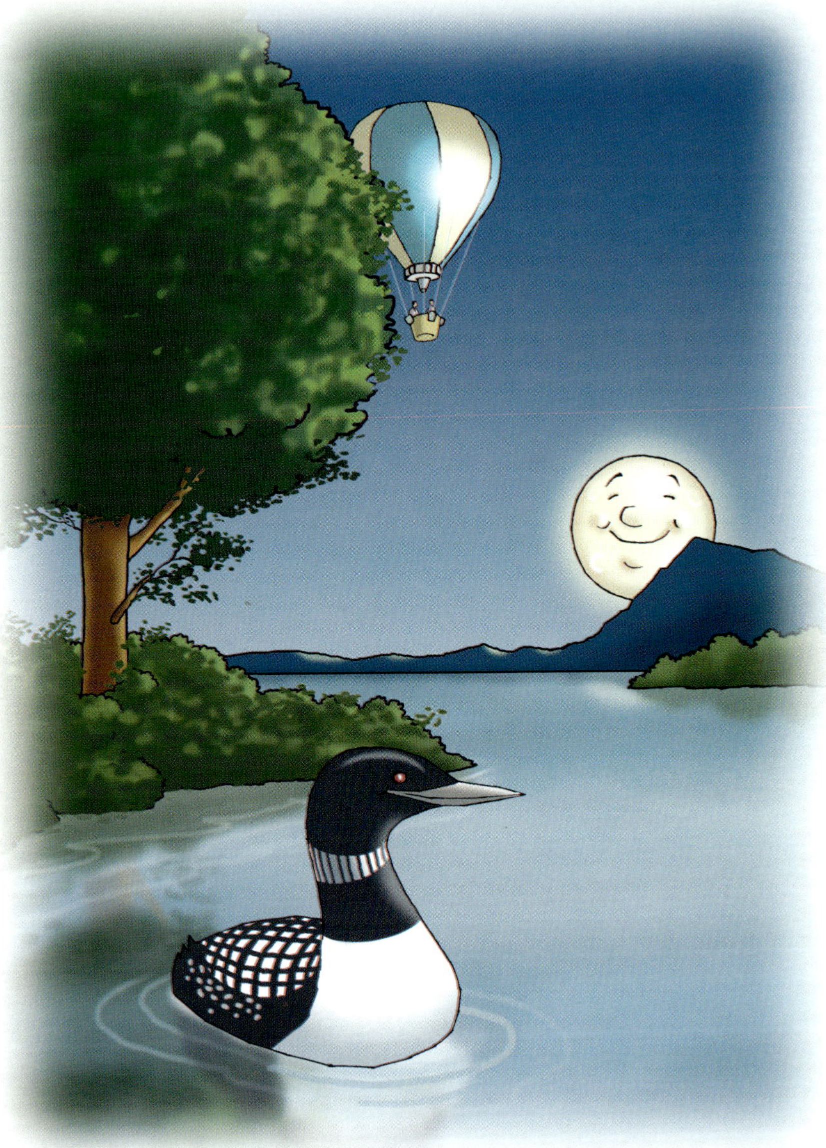

There's a loon with the Moon!

Mm

There's a moose with a goose!

Nn

There's a nuthatch in a blueberry patch!

Oo

There's an otter with a potter!

Pp

There's a p**ig** with a w**ig**!

There's a quail with a tail!

Rr

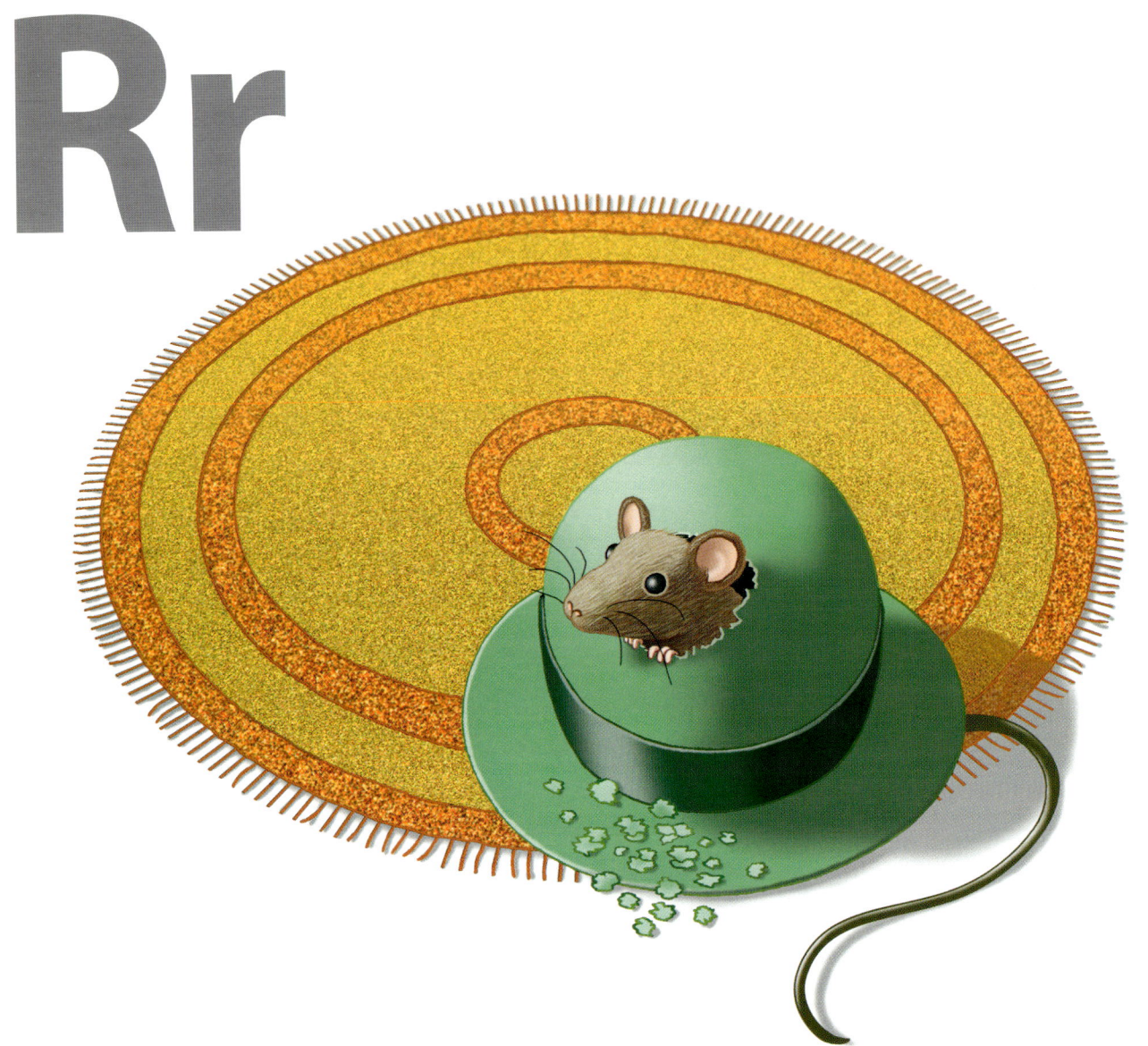

There's a rat in a hat!

Ss

There's a sn**ake** with a r**ake**!

Tt

There's a tern on a fern!

Uu

There's a unicorn with a horn!

Vv

There's a vole in a hole!

Ww

There's a weasel on a diesel!

Xx

There's an x-ray fish with a dish!

Yy

There's a yak in the flak!

Zz

There's a zebra in the umbra!

Parent-Teacher Guide to the Book

By Beth Williams, M.Ed., Curriculum and Instruction, Specialty in Early Childhood Education

This unique book encourages parents and teachers to use good teaching practices with beginning readers by using a combination of **patterned language**, **phonics**, and **high-frequency words**.

The book uses **patterned language** (similar sentence structure) which allows children to read the book independently and makes them feel confident in their early efforts to read.

The **phonics** aspect is included in the rhyming words and the "word family" spelling (meaning words that end in the same way; for example, cat and bat; goat and boat; loon and Moon).

There are **high-frequency words** (there's, a, an, in, the, on, the, with) which support a child's learning to spell the **high-frequency words**, as well as reinforcing a child's beginning reading.

Incorporating all three of the above teaching methods: **patterned language**, **phonics**, and **high-frequency words** when teaching children how to read helps them better understand how written language works and helps them become better readers.

Ideas for Using This Book:

Before Reading:

- Do a "picture walk" with the child and talk about the illustrations and what the text might say. Say some of the words that the child may not know (gorse, loo, umbra, etc.).

- Talk about the **patterned language** which the book uses. It may help the child to read the first page to him or her.

During Reading:

- Support reading by encouraging the child to use strategies to figure out unknown words, such as:
    - look at the illustration
    - make the first sound of a word
    - think about the word family (-at, -og, -ig)
    - make sure that what is read sounds right, looks right, and makes sense.

After Reading:

- Use tally marks to count the number of times each **high-frequency word** is used; for example, a, an, in, on, the, with.

- Encourage children to make a book of their own following the **pattern** used in this book, or a pattern similar to it.

- Copy a sentence from the book onto a piece of paper. As the child reads each word, cut the words apart. Have the child recreate the sentence using the words. This supports the child's understanding of words and spaces.

- Have the child identify other rhyming words seen in the illustrations (see Key to Rhyming Words in Each Illustration on page 4). These may be written down so that the child can see the **pattern** at the end of the rhyming words (**phonics**).

Acknowledgments

Thanks to Kathryn Wuebker, reading specialist, Loudoun County School System, Virginia, for reviewing the manuscript and making the recommendation to use red letters for the rhyming sounds in the words. I am grateful to Carol Chittenden, owner of Eight Cousins Children's Books, Falmouth, Massachusetts, for her advice and encouragement. Special thanks go to Kolbrún Hjaltadóttir, elementary school computer specialist, Reykjavík, Iceland, for recommending Bodvar Leos as the illustrator. I am especially thankful for the assistance of my wife and best friend, Mary Ellen Williams, former Spanish teacher, University of Michigan High School, Ann Arbor, Michigan, for her continual support, multiple reviews of the book, and recommendations for improvement. Lastly, I would like to give a special tribute to my great uncle, Frederic G. Melcher, President, R.R. Bowker Company, New York, and originator of the Caldecott Medal and Newbery Medal for children's books, who was a wonderful role model and supporter during my youth.